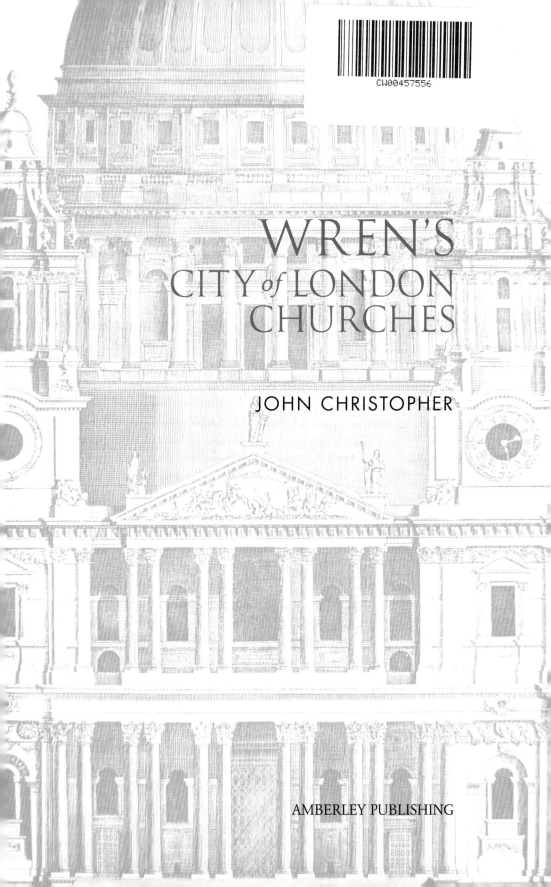

WREN'S
CITY *of* LONDON
CHURCHES

JOHN CHRISTOPHER

AMBERLEY PUBLISHING

As Surveyor of the King's Works from 1669 to 1718, Sir Christopher Wren was responsible for the rebuilding of fifty-one churches in the City of London, plus St Paul's Cathedral, following the Great Fire. He also worked on a number of other significant commissions including royal palaces at Kensington and Hampton Court, and the royal hospitals at Chelsea and Greenwich. Born in 1632, he died at the age of ninety in 1723.

First published 2012

Amberley Publishing
The Hill, Stroud
Gloucestershire, GL5 4EP

www.amberley-books.com

Copyright © John Christopher , 2012

The right of John Christopher to be identified as the Author of this work has been asserted in accordance with the Copyrights, Designs and Patents Act 1988.

ISBN 978 1 4456 0250 9

British Library Cataloguing in Publication Data. A catalogue record for this book is available from the British Library.

Typeset in 9.5pt on 12pt Celeste.
Typesetting by Amberley Publishing.
Printed in the UK.

Introduction: Born of fire

Shortly after midnight on the morning of Sunday 2 September 1666, a fire broke out at a bakery in Pudding Lane on the east side of the old City of London – the area contained within the Roman city walls. Such incidents were not uncommon and were usually dealt with swiftly by using fire hooks, lots of water and the more drastic measure of creating fire-breaks by demolishing adjoining properties. Unfortunately, London was tinder dry after a long drought and fed by a strong easterly wind, the blaze quickly spread. Sir Thomas Bloodworth, the Lord Mayor, was called upon to take command of the situation but by all accounts this yes-man was incapable of decisive action, in particular authorising the demolitions quickly enough to be effective. Through his incompetence the fire quickly leapt from one building to the next in the narrow streets. That night the fire was whipped up by the wind into an unstoppable fire-storm where the upward rush of hot air sucking in oxygen made it burn at temperatures high enough to melt church bells and cremate anyone unfortunate enough to be caught in its path. By the next day, Monday, the fire was pushing northwards into the heart of the City. There was utter chaos as thousands of Londoners attempted to flee as their homes and property came under threat. The streets were clogged with carts piled high with belongings and further impeding efforts to fight the fire as people headed for the medieval gateways in the old city walls. Many vented their anger on any unfortunate foreigners they came across as the rumours spread that the fires were being deliberately started by England's enemies.

Old St Paul's Cathedral engulfed by flames during the Great Fire of 1666. (*University of Toronto*)

Above: Detail of the 'wedding cake' spire of St Bride's, Fleet Street, the tallest of Wren's City churches.

Below: The magnificent dome of St Paul's Cathedral reflected in the glass walls of a modern shopping development.

By the end of the third day, Tuesday, the blaze had spread across most of the City. It engulfed St Paul's Cathedral, which was covered by wooden scaffolding because it was undergoing restoration under the direction of Christopher Wren, and driven by the gales it leapt across the River Fleet and even threatened the court at the Palace of Whitehall. Then the wind shifted, saving some of the buildings in the west but now putting the east side of the city in danger. The garrison at the Tower of London took matters into their own hands and used gunpowder to blow-up a huge number of houses, action which halted the advancing flames as the wind began to drop at last.

At the time of the Great Fire, London was the biggest city in England, its population more than the next fifty towns put together, and thousands of people now flocked to the impromptu encampments which had sprung up at Parliament Hill, Moorfields and Islington. The diarist Samuel Pepys recorded his impression of the scene. 'Poor wretches carrying their goods there, and every body keeping his goods together by themselves.' The colossal material destruction accounted for a staggering 13,000 houses, eighty-seven parish churches, forty-four Company Halls and a number of public buildings, including the Royal Exchange, the Custom House and St Paul's Cathedral.

It is thought that Christopher Wren had been in Oxford when the fire broke out and that he quickly returned to London. His father was another Christopher Wren, a rector at East Knoyle in Wiltshire and later Dean of Windsor. The younger Wren had studied Latin and the works of Aristotle at Oxford, where he came into contact with some equally stimulating minds. His own scientific interests embraced a broad spectrum of interests ranging from astronomy and optics to mechanics, microscopy, medicine, meteorology, and surveying. The latter broadly covered architecture, although as a profession this did not exist as we know it today and was seen by scientifically-minded gentlemen as being an extension of their interest in applied mathematics and geometry. Appointed Professor of Astronomy at Gresham College in London in 1657, and at Oxford in 1661, he was instrumental in the formation of the Royal Society in 1662 and later served as its president. Not only brilliant, Christopher Wren was also well connected. His uncle Matthew Wren was the Bishop of Ely and he gave him his first commission, building the great chapel at Pembroke College, Cambridge, which was consecrated in 1665. At around this time Wren was already involved with repairing and redesigning the old St Paul's Cathedral (see page 81). After the Great Fire, Wren's plans for a radical rebuild of the City were not adopted (see Wren's other London on page 87) but he was placed in charge of rebuilding fifty-one of the churches and, of course, St Paul's itself.

Above: Paternoster Square in the heart of the financial area, seen from the dome of St Paul's. The column pays a passing resemblance to The Monument, but it is in fact only a ventilation shaft. (*Gren*)

Many of Wren's churches are being over-shadowed by modern buildings. St Margaret Pattens in Eastcheap is next to the 20 Fenchurch Street office block, which will be wider towards the top.

The churches presented a number of challenges. In particular, he was to rebuild on the footprints of the medieval structures, usually incorporating their foundations, which resulted in irregular-shaped sites which were frequently hemmed in by other buildings. This accounts for the variety of layouts in the Wren churches, ranging from those with central domes and a Greek cross floor plan, to the rectangular form without aisles – the most common – and the conventional central nave with side aisles. Where possible they followed an east–west orientation with the altar at the eastern end and tower positioned on the western side, although there are exceptions to this. Wren also put great emphasis on his churches being 'Auditories' in which the congregation could both hear and see the service and sermon. This explains why so many were galleried, although to some extent this was also necessary to accommodate congregations swollen by the amalgamation of parishes.

Stylistically, Wren is widely heralded as being the father of English Baroque, a toned-down version of the overblown Baroque architecture found on the Continent and characterised by its penchant for the classical. Internally, Wren's City churches are usually very plain decoratively, leaving the architecture and furnishings to do the talking. His favoured window shape was the dome-headed with clear glass. (It was the Victorians who introduced the gaudy stained glass now seen in several of the 'beautified' or restored churches.) The use of building materials was sometimes determined by budgetary constraints, but nonetheless Wren was masterful, almost playful, in the juxtaposition of brick, Portland stone and stucco. However, it was with the steeples, the sum of the towers, domes, lanterns and spires, that he gave imagination full reign, from the pepper pot domes to the hexagonal cascade of Fleet Street's spectacular 'wedding cake'. It is also the steeples that bring us to a more contentious aspect of Wren's City churches. In many cases they were added after the main body of a church had been completed, sometimes several years later, and it seems clear that at least some of them were designed by his assistants, in particular Nicholas Hawksmoor. Certainly Robert Hooke had a hand in some of the churches, but given the amount of work that Wren's office was over-seeing, not to mention his other on-going commissions, this is hardly surprising.

For the most part, the City churches had been completed by 1700 and were followed by St Paul's in 1710, by which time Wren was seventy-eight years old. He had been knighted in 1673, married twice and reached the age of ninety by the time he died in February 1723. Of his City churches, twenty-nine have survived, if you include those which are towers only or tower and ruins. The poet Sir John Betjeman, an enthusiastic admirer of architecture, observed that 'Wren's cheerful genius pervades the whole City even today.'

List of Churches

Survivors, including rebuilt and towers only

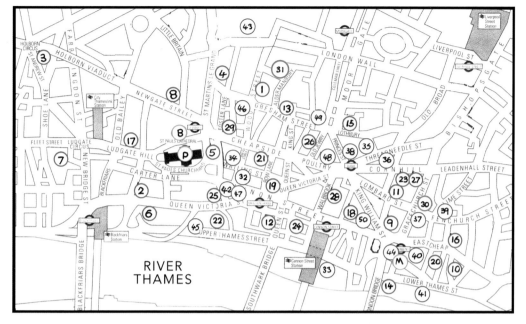

● Surviving Churches, including Towers or Ruins

● Relocated

● Lost Churches

Visiting Wren's City Churches

Most of the surviving churches are open to visitors, but please note that the majority are still active places of worship and hold services or recitals during weekdays as well as at weekends. The opening times for individual churches vary and many will have visitor information on their websites, but in at least one case you do need to make arrangements with the church in advance. Most permit photography, although St Paul's Cathedral emphatically does not, and it is only good manners to ask for permission first. Enjoy visiting Wren's remaining churches. You will be warmly welcomed, but please respect the privacy and quiet of others.

As can be seen from the map, the churches are bunched fairly close together, all within walking distance of another. The Friends of the City Churches organise special City Church Walks during the year, and their members are also involved in keeping the churches open to visitors. See www.london-city-churches.org.uk for more information.

Dwarfed by modern buildings on three sides, the tower is all that remains of St Alban, Wood Street. The body of the church was destroyed in the Blitz.

St Alban, Wood Street

1 Tower only. Location: Wood Street.

A lone tower in a canyon of concrete and glass, St Alban is perhaps not characteristic of Wren's work as it is firmly rooted in the Gothic. Records of a church on this site date back to the eleventh century, but by the sixteenth it had become dilapidated, being rebuilt in 1634 only to be destroyed in the Great Fire of 1666. Wren's replacement, completed in 1685, is illustrated in *Parentalia*, an account of his life and work by his son, yet another Christopher Wren. This shows a handsome building which echoes its pre-Fire Gothic appearance with high, pointed windows. These were not to the liking of Wren Jnr, who commented that 'there is something wanting in the respect of apertures, for the body of the church within is not sufficiently enlightened'. The most striking feature of St Alban was the tower, which stood within the north-west corner of the church. Ninety-two feet tall to the tip of its pinnacles, the tower is in four stages with a large widow in the lower one, then circular and round-arched apertures in the next two, plus bell apertures in the upper stage. This tower is all that remains as the main building was damaged in the 1940 Blitz and finally demolished in 1965. It has since been converted into a private residence.

The distinctive redbrick and contrasting stone of St Andrew-by-the-Wardrobe on Queen Victoria Street. Its name comes from the Royal Wardrobe, which was located just above the church.

St Andrew's Wardrobe Puddle Dock Hill.

St Andrew-by-the-Wardrobe

2 Blitzed, rebuilt. Location: Queen Victoria Street.

In deep red brick edged with contrasting stone, St Andrew-by-the-Wardrobe is a striking building. Its distinctive name comes from the Royal Wardrobe, a storehouse for the Crown's arms and clothing located just to the north of the church until the Great Fire. The church is situated on St Andrew's Hill, an imposing and uncluttered setting when seen from Queen Victoria Street, and was rebuilt in 1695, making it one of the last City churches by Wren. The interior is aisled with five arcaded bays supported by piers with galleries all round and a screen beneath the west gallery. Above the aisles the ceiling is vaulted and over the nave it is barrel-roofed, decorated with plasterwork of wreaths and cherubs. Minor changes have been made over the years – in particular the central entrance was moved to the east side of the tower in the 1820s. Totally gutted in the Blitz of 1940, the interior was restored by Marshall Sisson between 1959-61, with many fittings coming from other churches. For example the pulpit came from St Matthew, Friday Street, and the Royal Arms from St Olave, Old Jewry. The weathervane is from St Michael Bassishaw, which was demolished in 1900. Its most famous former parishioner was William Shakespeare when he was working at the Blackfriars Theatre and had a house in the parish.

St Andrew, Holborn, stands apart from the City churches and escaped the Great Fire. In poor repair, Wren rebuilt the church retaining the fifteenth-century tower.

14

St Andrew, Holborn

③ Rebuilt by Wren. Location: Holborn Viaduct.

Situated just outside the north-western edge of the old city walls, but within 'the Liberty', St Andrew is the largest of Wren's parish churches and is a little removed from the others. The old medieval church had escaped the flames of 1666 thanks to a last minute change in the wind direction; however, it was in such a poor state of repair that the main part was rebuilt from the foundations upwards. Wren kept the fifteenth-century tower, which was re-faced around 1704, and it was around this time that the bulbous pinnacles, originally capped by weathervanes, were also added. Although the church was gutted by enemy bombers during the Second World War on the night of 7 May 1941, the interior has been lovingly restored to Wren's original designs. This lofty space is bright and airy with its white barrel-vaulted ceiling supported on Corinthian columns and decorated with coloured and gilded plasterwork. There are wooden panelled galleries bathed in the light which streams in through two rows of clear glass windows, especially through the tall, round-headed upper ones. Note the stained glass window in the east window, the marble font and also the gilded organ case given by Handel to the Foundling's Hospital in 1750. The figurines on either side of the front entrance represent children from the former Parish School.

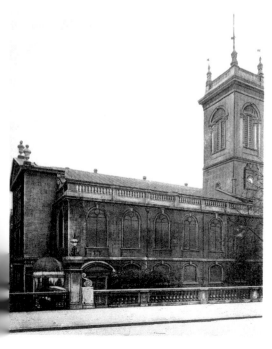

The redbrick elevations of St Anne and St Agnes stand out among the grey commercial building of Gresham Street. Curiously, the building varies in detail from the engraving published in Wren Jnr's *Parentalia*, shown opposite. The church was gutted in the Blitz and restored in the 1960s.

St Anne and St Agnes

4 Blitzed, rebuilt. Location: Gresham Street.

Located near the Barbican, references to a church variously referred to as St Anne or St Agnes, thanks to its unusual double dedication, date back to the twelfth century. It was destroyed by fire for the first time in 1548, then again in 1666 when just the tower survived, to be gutted for a third time in the Blitz of December 1940. It is a small church with an unusual ground plan based on a Greek cross. On three elevations, it features a central pedimented gable with a high round-headed window flanked by smaller windows to either side. John Betjeman once described it as 'a refreshing red brick interlude in the modern mediocrity of Gresham Street', although strictly speaking the north side has been stuccoed. Using a similar formula to that at St Martin Ludgate and St Mary-at-Hill, Wren devised a vaulted square roof supported by Corinthian columns. His tower incorporated the first two stages of the fourteenth-century tower, and is a squat 84 feet, including the square lantern. The tower has also been stuccoed and seen from the far side it looks like it doesn't belong with the rest of the building. The church was restored in the 1960s and is now used by the Lutherans. Former parishioners include John Milton, John Bunyan and John Wesley, the founder of Methodism.

The Parish Church of St Anne Within Alders-Gate

Above: The slender tower of St Augustine, Watling Street, is now incorporated within the Cathedral Choir School.

Below and left: Despite the attention of modern arsonists, St Benet, Paul's Wharf, is one of the few Wren churches to have survived intact.

St Augustine, Watling Street

5 Tower only. Location: Cannon Street/New Change.

Easily overshadowed, St Augustine is a former Anglican church located on the north side of Watling Street, immediately to the east of Wren's great cathedral. It is sometimes referred to as St Augustine Old Change or Budge Row. After the 1666 Fire, the rebuilding of the main part was completed by 1684, in a plain and modest style, with the tower finished by 1696 – almost thirty years after the fire. In three stages, this simple oblong tower is crowned by a pierced balustrade, with corner obelisk pinnacles, which encircles the lead-covered lantern and slender steeple. Thought to have been designed by Nicholas Hawksmoor, the tower has an overall height of around 145 feet. The spire was altered in 1830 to give it a heavier point, but the present one more closely matches the original. Internally, the body of the church was divided into a nave and six aisles by Corinthian columns supporting a barrel-vaulted ceiling. In 1941 the entire church was destroyed by the enemy bombings and with the construction of the St Paul's Cathedral Choir School, between 1962–67, only the tower was rebuilt to be incorporated within the modern school building.

St Benet, Paul's Wharf

6 Survived. Location: White Lion Hill.

Standing on the slope down to the riverside, St Benet is unusual in that it is one of only four churches by Wren – although widely attributed to Robert Hooke – to have survived intact. However, it only narrowly escaped destruction in the late nineteenth century when the parish was merged with St Nicholas Cole Abbey. Saved by a campaign, it has been the Welsh Church of the City of London since 1879 and services in Welsh are held every Sunday. In 1971 vandals set fire to the church and although the direct damage was restricted to the north-east corner, the heat damage was more widespread. A restoration programme was carried out over the following two years. Often described as being in a Dutch style, St Benet is in red and blue brick with contrasting stone quoins and cornice, plus decorative festoons above the rounded windows of clear glass. Inside it retains its galleries, alter and pulpit. The brick-built tower is capped with a modest lead sheathed dome and turret. It is a pity that the architects of the London College next door copied the brick colour from St Benet. Their aim may have been to blend in with the church, but the result is that the church is a little lost against the redbrick backdrop.

The 226-foot spire of St Bride's, Fleet Street, makes it the tallest of Wren's City churches. For obvious reasons it has earned the nickname of the 'wedding cake' church.

St Bride's, Fleet Street

7 Blitzed, rebuilt. Location: Fleet Street.

Originally known as St Bridget's, it is thought that a church has been here since the eighth century, possibly with Saxon or Roman foundations. St Bride's is one of Wren's finest churches and has the advantage of standing on higher ground to the south of Fleet Street. It is affectionately referred to as the 'wedding cake' church, not just for the associations with its name but also for the steeple of five diminishing octagons. At 226 feet high, it is the tallest of all of Wren's steeples and he clearly lavished great attention on the rebuilding of St Bride's. The main body of the church took seven years to complete, by 1684 (the steeple was not added until 1701–03). It has five bays with double Tuscan columns supporting a barrel vault, pierced at intervals by circular clerestory windows. The side aisles are groin vaulted. Sadly, the interior was gutted in the Blitz, especially so as it has been described as 'magnificent'. It was restored by Godfrey Allen in the 1950s with some remodelling, including the replacement of the galleries with stalls running east–west, plus a new altarpiece bringing the east end forward. The inset stained glass oval window might be a little bit intrusive, but Glyn Jones's Trompe l'Oeil painting effectively conveys the illusion of a curved wall beyond.

St Bride's was extensively damaged during the air raids of the Second World War. The interior was restored in the 1950s with some remodelling of the layout.

Wren's second tallest spire is at Christ Church, Greyfriars. The main body of the church was all but destroyed in the Blitz, although the tower remains as a very expensive private residence.

Christf Church, Greyfriars

8 Tower only. Location: Newgate Street.

Another church with a magnificent steeple, Christ Church Greyfriars – sometimes known as Christchurch Newgate Street – is located a little to the north of St Paul's. The original church was in the Gothic style, but was rebuilt post-Fire in the English Baroque by Wren and was described by his son as 'spacious and beautiful'. The old foundations were partially reused and the new church, minus a steeple at that point, was completed in 1687. The tower was finally finished in 1704 and had an arched main entranceway, windows above, with neoclassical pediments and large bell shutters. Working upwards, it boasted just about every decorative element at Wren's disposal, including ornamental pineapples plus lanterns enclosed by twelve vases. Overall it is 153 feet high, making it second only to St Bride's. Within the church the nave had two rows of columns with elaborate capitals, running east–west, with pilasters – flat representations of columns – on the end walls. On 29 December 1940 Christ Church was hit by a fire-bomb and the flames tore though the interior. The tower and side walls survived and a public garden has been created on the site. In 2006, the tower was converted into a twelve-storey private residence and at the time of publishing it was being offered for sale at a cool $4.5 million.

St Clement in Eastcheap gives a good idea of how the City churches were often hemmed in among the other buildings. The interior was fiddled with by the Victorians, but thankfully they retained the seventeenth-century canopied pulpit.

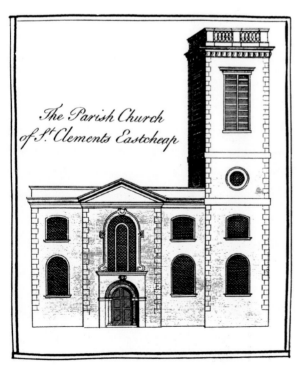

The Parish Church of St Clements Eastcheap

St Clement, Eastcheap

9 Survived. Location: Clement's Lane.

Was this the church that inspired the line, 'Oranges and lemons ring the bell of St Clement's'? (The only other candidate is St Clement Danes.) It is a pleasing church tucked away in Clement's Lane in Eastcheap – the word 'cheap' derived from the Saxon meaning market. Despite being cheek-by-jowl with neighbouring buildings, the simple interior, illuminated by two rows of round-topped windows on the south wall, plus high clerestory windows along one side, is not as dark as might be expected and is surprisingly spacious. After the Fire it was rebuilt in 1686, by which time the parish had been combined with St Martin Orgar on the south side of Eastcheap. Wren's building is on an irregular site with the south aisle tapered. Note the elaborate seventeenth-century hexagonal canopied pulpit and also the fine organ casing, although the organ itself has been repeatedly rebuilt. In 1872 William Butterfield 'renovated' the interior, which included removing the galleries and moving the organ. The ceiling was renewed in 1925 and its central panels painted dark blue with gilded embellishments. The tower, aligned with the street and not the church itself, is very plain, capped with only a simple balustrade and no spire. Betjeman describes the church as modest and unpretentious while Pevsner calls it unassuming – both complimentary, if taken in context.

St Dunstan-in-the-East was repaired by Wren, who added the unusual buttressed steeple. In 1941 the Luftwaffe gutted the main building and the ruins are now a public garden.

St Dunstan-in-the-East

⑩ Blitzed, tower/ruins. Location: St Dunstan's Hill.

Situated on St Dunstan's Hill, St Dunstan-in-the-East is the most easterly of Wren's City churches although, in truth, it was never really a Wren church. The original church was built around 1100 and although damaged in the Great Fire, it was repaired in 1668–71 rather than rebuilt. Wren's main contribution to its appearance is the unusual steeple consisting of four smaller spires on the corners plus four flying buttresses arching upwards to support the principle spire. This was only added in 1698 and designed in the Gothic style by Wren, probably with assistance from Nicholas Hawksmoor, to match the rest of the building. By the early nineteenth century the church was in need of a major refurbishment and this was carried out by David Laing between 1817–21. Amazingly, Wren's unusual steeple survived the Blitz intact, but the main body of the church was gutted in 1941. After the war it was decided not to rebuild St Dunstan's and the ruins were converted into a public garden, which opened in 1971. Of the main body of the church only the north and south walls, plus the shell of the porch on the north-east side, remain. The tower still stands tall and proud and is home to the All Hallows House Foundation, a local charity. Occasional open-air services are conducted in the gardens.

St Edmund, King-and-Martyr, has a fine symmetrical frontage on Lombard Street. The stained glass has made the interior a little gloomy, and the pews have given way to bookshelves.

St Edmund, King-and-Martyr

⓫ Now London Centre for Spirituality. Location: Lombard Street.

Not one of the bigger churches, St Edmund's nave was just 69 feet long with a width of 39 feet. It has been suggested that it was most probably designed by Robert Hooke. Unusually, the altar was placed at the north end of the nave – as it had been on the pre-Fire building – rather than on the eastern side, which is the norm. In *Parentalia*, Christopher Wren Jnr explained why: 'This singular and inconvenient shape of the body is owing to the value of ground in front in that part of the town, and the steeple, which consists of tower and spire, is equally singular.' He didn't stop there. 'There is also an unpleasing openness in the arches of the lanthorn.' In 1864, the *Illustrated London News* proclaimed it to be 'Wren's worst church', but balance was restored by John Betjeman, who described the front of the church as 'a handsome Portland stone composition'. Architectural taste does change with time and the Victorians have to answer for the stained glass windows above the altar. The projecting clock was added around 1810. During the First World War, the building was damaged in an air raid. Today it is still a consecrated church and since 2001 it serves as the London Centre for Spirituality, with the pews replaced by bookshelves.

St James, Garlickhythe, is an imposing church at the bottom of Garlick Hill overlooking Upper Thames Street. The spire is thought to be by Nicholas Hawksmoor, and the fine clock is a replica of the 1682 original.

St James, Garlickhythe

⑫ Survived. Location: Garlick Hill.

Sometimes known as 'Wren's lantern' because of its profusion of windows, St James Garlickhythe is named after the disciple St James, plus 'hythe' for the landing place on the river where the French ships brought their garlic and wine. There have been references to a church here since the twelfth century under a variety of names, including St James in the Vintry, St James Comyns and St James-by-the-Thames. This was an important church, as indicated by the burial of six Lord Mayors here in the Middle Ages, and the building was repaired and expanded several times before the Great Fire. Wren's church is a rectangle with a tower at the western end. The tower is of brick and was partially stuccoed originally, being faced with Portland stone after the Second World War. It is in three stages, surmounted by a Hawksmoor spire in a style similar to those on St Stephen Walbrook and St Michael Paternoster. The entrance used to be on the north wall. Inside, there is a tall nave with vaulted ceiling, plus side aisles and two rows of Ionic columns, and the transepts were originally arranged north–south by Wren. The church was bombed in the Blitz and then hit by a falling crane in 1991. It has since been sympathetically restored. The clock is a modern replica of the 1682 original.

The wider view of St Lawrence Jewry reveals a handsome and substantial building which is now the official church of the City of London Corporation.

St Lawrence Jewry

13 Blitzed, rebuilt. Location: Gresham Street.

This imposing free-standing church on Gresham Street and the Guildhall Yard is now the official church of the City of London Corporation. It was originally built in the twelfth century, near the former Jewish ghetto which was centred on Old Jewry. When rebuilt after the Great Fire, between 1670 and 1687, it was surrounded by other buildings, which explains why the side walls are fairly plain, but the Luftwaffe has since reorganised the area to expose the wider view. It is stone faced and the east front in particular is very imposing, with four Corinthian columns supporting a classical podium. The tower has a balustraded parapet with corner obelisks rising above the four-sided bell chamber. Wren Jnr was unfairly critical of the spire, which he described as 'low and not very elegant', whereas Betjeman summed up St Lawrence Jewry as 'very splendid'. The present spire is a glass-fibre replica of the leaded original. The interior is a generous rectangular space illuminated by tall round-headed windows and clerestory windows above. Entering through the west end beneath the tower, you pass under the wooden organ case and through a screen supported on heavy wooden pillars. None of this is original as St Lawrence was gutted in the 1940 bombings and restored in the 1950s by Cecil Brown in-keeping with Wren's original.

Set back slightly from the Thames, St Magnus the Martyr was modified in the eighteenth century to improve the access to London Bridge. Today, the river can only be glimpsed through a gap between the drab office buildings. The best view of the church is from The Monument, shown opposite.

St Magnus the Martyr

14 Altered. Location: Lower Thames Street.

Nestling between modern office buildings beside the Thames, St Magnus the Martyr is one of my favourite Wren churches, with its domed octagonal tower looking like a chess piece. A church has been here since the twelfth century, dedicated to St Magnus, Earl of Orkney, who apparently never was martyred for his religious beliefs. A stone's throw from the Monument and Pudding Lane, it was one of the first churches to be engulfed by the Great Fire. It was rebuilt by Wren in 1676 and the steeple, copied from St Charles Borromée in Antwerp, was added some thirty years later. After another fire damaged the western end of the church and several buildings on the Old London Bridge in 1760, it was decided to widen the approaches to the bridge to ease the terrible congestion. The two most western of the nine bays of the church were demolished between 1762 and 1768, although the tower was retained, with the newly exposed base opened out to allow a walkway to pass through it. Further modifications were made to the main body of the building over the ensuing years and the interior was restored in the 1920s to a neo-Baroque style. It is galleried, with barrel-vaulting supported on Ionic columns, and lit by oval clerestory windows. The clock protruding from the tower is dated 1709.

Located behind the Bank of England, St Margaret Lothbury is noted for its wonderful wood carving such as the chancel screen above, much of which has been donated by other Wren churches.

St Margaret Lothbury

⑮ Survived. Location: Lothbury.

Tucked behind the Bank of England, St Margaret Lothbury is characterised by its slender tower and an intimate interior brimming with sumptuous woodwork donated by other churches. After the Great Fire, Wren rebuilt St Margaret between 1686 and 1690. Based on a skewed floor plan, it has a central nave plus a single aisle to the south side separated by Corinthian columns, with corresponding pilasters on the north wall. It is mostly illuminated by three tall, round-headed windows onto the street plus further circular clerestory windows on either side of the coved ceiling. The beautifully carved chancel screen running across the nave came from All-Hallows-the-Great, which was demolished in 1894, and it is one of only two examples of surviving Wren screens in the City churches; the other being at St Peter upon Cornhill. The altarpiece was restored by Rodney Tatchell after the war and this is flanked by paintings from St Christopher-le-Stocks (demolished in 1781). The base of the south aisle screen and also the communion tables all come from St Olave Jewry, while the large tester – the wooden canopy over the pulpit – is another donation from All-Hallows-the-Great. The church tower is in four stages, with a fine pedimented entrance at its base and a spire in the form of an obelisk sitting atop a four-sided dome.

The Parish Church of St Margaret Pattens in Little Tower Street

Such is the rate of development in this part of London that some of the buildings shown in the photograph above have already disappeared to make way for the new 20 Fenchurch Street development. (*John Armagh*)

St Margaret Pattens

16 Survived. Location: Eastcheap.

St Margaret Pattens in Eastcheap is dedicated to St Margaret of Antioch, with its suffix supposedly derived from the local pattenmakers who made wooden-soled overshoes worn by Londoners to keep their feet out of the muck and mud on the streets. This post-Fire church was completed in 1687 and is one of the few to escape significant damage in the Blitz. Its most notable feature is the 200-foot-high polygonal spire – Wren's third highest – sheathed in lead. It is sometimes described as his only true spire as it is spared the pyramids, lanterns and turrets favoured on many of the others. The church faces on to Rood Lane with a fine façade; a large, round-headed central window above the doorway, flanked by two smaller ones, each beneath a circular window. These portholes are the punctuation marks on many of Wren's churches and the tower has them on its first three stages. Inside, the main body is oblong, with galleries plus an aisle on the north side. Note the huge monument hanging on the south wall, also the canopied pews dating from the seventeenth century and intended for the churchwardens. For those who misbehaved there was another seat, a punishment box carved with the Devil's head. The church is anticipating being overshadowed by the new 20 Fenchurch Street development.

The dark spire of St Martin on Ludgate Hill dissects the west face of St Paul's on the approach from Fleet Street. The viaduct shown in the old postcard *c.* 1900, opposite, is no longer there.

St Martin, Ludgate

17 Survived. Location: Ludgate Hill.

One of the last churches to be rebuilt after the Great Fire, St Martin Ludgate rises conspicuously on the approach from Fleet Street towards St Paul's. The Portland stone façade is symmetrical with a central tower, projecting slightly, which has two tall stages. The entrance is beneath a high, curve-headed window on the first, and there are bell shutters on the upper one. The curved stone elements linking the main body of the church to the tower, much like an inverted buttress, are known as volutes and are mimicked in a smaller scale at the top of the tower. Above that is a heavy stone cornice, a hexagonal stone base or stage and then the convex hexagonal leaded dome, iron balcony and spire. The building is aligned north–south, but once inside the nave is orientated east–west and separated from the street front by three hefty arches. The central square roof space is supported on four white columns beneath another deep cornice. The base of the columns and the surrounding walls are panelled in dark wood. St Martin sustained only minor damage during the Blitz and many internal features are original, including the pulpit and the reredos, the carved screen behind the altar. Note the seventeenth-century bread shelves, originally from St Mary Magdelen, where bread from the wealthy would be kept for redistribution to poorer parishioners.

St Mary Abchurch is a hidden gem among the hustle and bustle of the City. The brick exterior is unpretentious, but inside the real surprise is the glorious dome, painted by William Snow in 1708.

St Mary Abchurch

18 Survived. Location: Abchurch Lane.

This is one of my favourite Wren churches. The previous church building was destroyed in the Great Fire and rebuilt in 1681–86. Amid the hustle and bustle there is a small open area, the former churchyard, beside the squarish church. The bricks and stone dressings have darkened with age and in style it has a lot in common with St Benet, Paul's Wharf. But like a special present, the real surprise is inside. Upon entering, the eye is immediately drawn upwards, above the dark woodwork of the panelled box pews, the carved door-cases and the fine Grinling Gibbons reredos or altarpiece, to where the dark painted dome springing from the four walls is illuminated by oval windows known as 'lunettes'. The painting, with its false perspective, was not of Wren's doing and is unique among his City churches. It is by William Snow, carried out when the building was 'beautified' in 1708, and depicts the Name of God in Hebrew surrounded by sun rays and angels. Badly damaged in the 1940 bombings, St Mary Abchurch was restored by Godfrey Allen between 1948–53 and the dome repainted by W. Hoyle. The tower, in four stages and capped by a pierced lantern with lead sheathed obelisk spire above, is almost hidden when viewed from Abchurch Yard and is best seen from the alleyway.

Wren rebuilt St Mary Aldermary, incorporating much of the surviving structure, which explains the strong Gothic flavour of the church and tower.

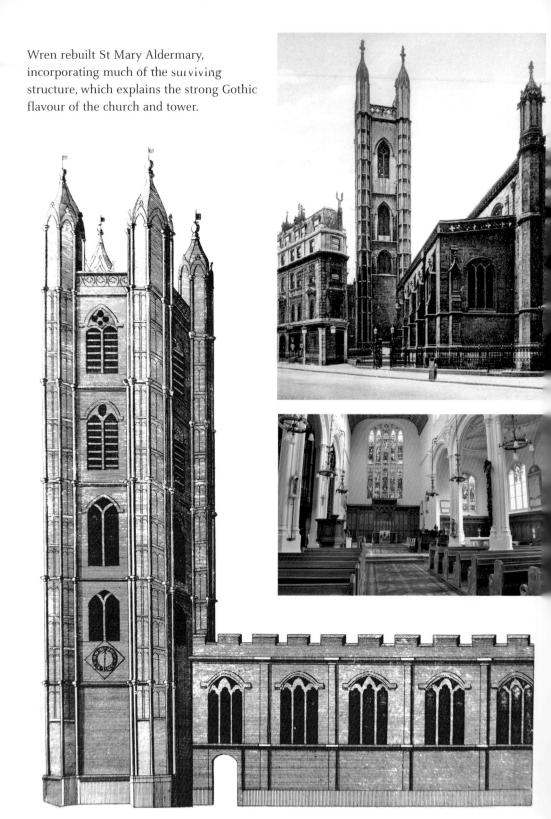

St Mary Aldermary

19 Survived. Location: Bow Lane.

A church has stood here on Bow Lane, near to Watling Street, for over 900 years. The name Adlermary is thought to denote that it is the oldest one dedicated to St Mary. A major rebuild commenced in the early sixteenth century was completed 100 years later, but the church was severely damaged in the Great Fire. It was rebuilt by Wren in 1679–82 using the surviving parts of the tower and walls. This explains why St Mary Aldermary is in the Gothic style, making it one of the least typical of his City churches. The body of the church is to a rectangular plan, with six bays plus north and south aisles beneath a clerestoried roof with a fan-vaulted ceiling intricately decorated in pristine icing-sugar white plasterwork. There was some damage to this plasterwork during the Blitz but since then the church has been restored many times. Unfortunately, the Wren furnishings were removed in the nineteenth century in pursuit of a more 'authentic' medieval interior. The lofty tower, 135 feet high, was not completed until 1704, and with its distinctive bottle-shaped corner pinnacles it remains a prominent landmark on the City skyline. Note the memorial to the lost church of St Antholin, Watling Street, situated near the north porch on the outside wall – see page 71.

By the nineteenth century concerns about public health meant that the crowded churchyards could no longer be used for burials.

Below: The interior of St Mary-at-Hill looks bare, but some of the wooden fittings have been in storage since the fire of 1988.

St Mary-at-Hill

20 Survived, rebuilt. Location: Lovat Lane.

This is another of Wren's square churches. There is a tower on Lovat Lane to the west, but the more visible stone façade looks eastwards, with a fine double-sided clock projecting out over St Mary-at-Hill. Its central window was blocked off in 1767. Betjeman says that St Mary had the 'least spoiled and the most gorgeous interior in the City', but at first sight it is a surprisingly empty space – a victim of de-cluttering, you might think. In fact, this church has endured a succession of fires and subsequent restorations: by George Gwilt in 1787–88, by James Savage in 1827 and again in 1848-49. The latest fire occurred in 1988, when the roof and interior were damaged; however, these have since been renovated. Inside, the body of the church is very airy, with a barrel-vault in a Greek cross plan and central dome, resting on free-standing Corinthian columns, rising above the flat ceiling. Much of the woodwork, including the organ case, has been carefully restored, although the church is without most of its pews. Alterations to the exterior have been many, including, for example, the fitting of round-headed windows in the early nineteenth century. At the turn of the nineteenth/twentieth century, the church was under the ministry of Wilson Carlile, the founder of the Church Army in 1882.

According to tradition a true Cockney must be born within earshot of the Bow bells. St Mary-le-Bow represents Wren on a grand scale, and although the lofty interior was gutted in the Blitz it is still very impressive.

St Mary-le-Bow

21 Blitzed, rebuilt. Location: Cheapside.

Famed for its bells – according to tradition, they persuaded Dick Whittington to turn back – the 224-foot steeple of St Mary-le-Bow makes this one of the most prominent of the churches in the City. This is Wren on a grand scale, although it is generally conceded that the body of the church was probably not his work. According to Pevsner, its crowning glory is the steeple, which is actually shorter than the one at St Bride's. The tower is of Portland stone, consisting of a tall lower stage, narrow central stage with iron balcony onto Cheapside, and bell stage with pairs of Ionic pilasters. Then comes a balustrade surrounding a rotunda and columns, another balustrade, volutes, and another rotunda, all finally culminating in a slender obelisk. It was as if Wren threw in every device at his disposal to make this the most ornate of all the steeples, and he succeeded. In comparison, the western brick façade of the body of the church seems an incongruous change of materials and style. The central bay has three round-headed windows, the largest over a central entrance, plus round or oval windows above. Inside, there is a high, barrel-vaulted ceiling in white and blue. Note the imposing organ case over the entrance. The interior was gutted during the Blitz and largely rebuilt by Laurence King after the war.

St Mary Somerset

22 Tower only. Location: Upper Thames Street.

After the Fire this was one of the last of the City churches to be rebuilt, finished in 1694. By all accounts this was a poor parish and the church was one of only two to be furnished from money coming from the Coal Tax. All that remains of St Mary Somerset today is the lonely tower, so we must rely on Christopher Wren Jnr's *Parentalia* for the bare bones of a description. 'Of stone, with the tower. Here are two aisles, with a flat roof, adorned with a cornice, and between the windows with fretwork of cherubims, etc. The length is 83ft, breadth 36ft, height 30ft and of the tower, to the top of highest pinnacles, 120ft.' The tower has eight of these pinnacles, unusually arranged with the taller obelisks rising halfway along each of its sides and stone vases on the corners. St Mary Somerset was not, as you might assume, a victim of the Blitz. It was deliberately demolished in 1871 as a result of the Union of Benefices Act of 1860 in response to the population drift away from the City. The parish was combined with St Nicholas Cole Abbey, not far away. Curiously, however, the tower was preserved standing on this awkward spot on Upper Thames Street and now has a small garden at its feet.

Another lone tower. St Mary Somerset was not a victim of the Blitz, however, as the church was demolished in 1871 as a result of the Union of Benefices Act of 1860.

The Gothic tower of St Michael,
Cornhill, survived the Great
Fire but was reconstructed in
the early eighteenth century
with pinnacles by Nicholas
Hawksmoor. The Wren interior,
opposite, reflects Victorian taste
following a restyling by Sir
George Gilbert Scott.

St Michael, Cornhill

23 Survived. Location: Cornhill.

St Michael is obscured from view by the other buildings on Cornhill, apart from a slender gap by the entrance. There has been a church here since medieval times and the present building is reminiscent of St Mary Aldermary with its Gothic tower and bottle-like pinnacles, but don't be deceived. After the Great Fire only the body of the church was rebuilt, between 1669 and 1672, as the tower remained intact. This in turn was reconstructed almost forty years later from 1715 to 1722, with a break in the proceeding when the funds dried up, and the more ornate bell stage and pinnacles are the work of Nicholas Hawksmoor, as Wren was ninety years old by this time. In the mid-nineteenth century, the church was given a thorough makeover in line with the Victorian taste for high Gothic, the interior restyled by Sir George Gilbert Scott, plus new stained glass and the addition of a decorative entrance porch. The body of the church is rectangular, with robust Tuscan columns supporting a barrel vaulted ceiling. During the Second World War the Luftwaffe failed to undo the Victorians' handiwork. The interior was restored in the 1960s and repainted in a more muted scheme, including pastel blue for the ceiling – a colour choice thoroughly disapproved of by the architectural purist John Betjeman.

The Parish Church of S.t Michael Royal College Hill.

St Michael, Paternoster Royal, is known as Dick Whittington's church and it is said that he was buried in the grounds. Today it is home to the Mission to Seafarers and the bright interior is enhanced by John Hayward's stained glass windows, including one depicting Whittington, above.

St Michael, Paternoster Royal

24 Blitzed, rebuilt. Location: College Street.

Dick Whittington lived next door and a plaque commemorates his burial in 1422, although some sources suggest it was 1423. His body was dug up on several occasions but the last attempt to locate it, in 1949, uncovered only a mummified cat. Wren's church, situated on College Hill, is on a rectangular plan with Portland stone facing and six round-headed windows with cherub keystones on the south front, and brick on the north and east. The tower, probably by Hawksmoor, is capped by two colonnaded open octagons plus stone spire. Before the Blitz a number of buildings obscured the view from the south, but subsequently the war-damaged buildings were cleared, revealing the view from Upper Thames Street. The church itself was hit by a V1 Doodlebug in 1944, with only walls and tower left standing. A proposal to demolish it, leaving just the tower, was rejected and the building was restored between 1966 and 1968. Today, the west side is used as offices by the Mission to Seafarers and their flags can be seen in the larger eastern part which forms the main body of the church. The plain white walls above the darker woodwork, including original reredos, are the perfect foil to several vividly coloured modern windows designed by John Hayward. Dick Whittington is portrayed in one of these.

St Nicholas Cole Abbey, on Victoria Street, features a distinctive spire in the form of an inverted octagonal trumpet or funnel, complete with balcony and oval lunettes.

St Nicholas, Cole Abbey

㉕ Blitzed, rebuilt. Location: Queen Victoria Street.

Cole Abbey is derived from the medieval term 'coldharbour', meaning a shelter for travellers, and the earliest references to a church are from the twelfth century. One of the first to be rebuilt after the Fire, it was completed by 1678 and the parish combined with St Nicholas Olave, which was not rebuilt. In *Parentalia* it is described as consisting of 'a well-proportioned body, and of a steeple composed of a spire very justly adapted to one another in form and proportion'. The main part is a solid-looking rectangular box with a row of six high, round-headed windows on the Portland stone south wall and a balustrade on top. The tower has a striking lead spire, described as an inverted octagonal trumpet, pierced by two rows of oval lunettes. Two-thirds up there is an iron crow's nest balcony, and to complete the nautical theme the vane is in the form of a three-masted barque, from St Michael Queenhithe (demolished 1876). Completely gutted in the 1941 Blitz, the church was not restored until the 1960s. The interior is fairly plain with a west gallery and screen. Most notable is the stained glass by Keith New. Originally, the south side was obscured by surrounding buildings, but the view was opened up by changes to the street plan in Victorian times, and by the Luftwaffe.

St Olave, Old Jewry is tucked away down the alleyways of this area of medieval London once populated by the Jewish community. It was demolished in 1892 and only the tower and part of the west wall remain.

The West Prospect of the Parish Church of S.t Olave in the Old Jewry

This fine doorway flanked by Doric columns is pure Wren. The tower is now incorporated within later office buildings.

St Olave, Old Jewry

㉖ Tower and west wall only. Location: Ironmonger Lane.

St Olave, or Olaf, is the eleventh-century patron saint of Norway, while Old Jewry – sometimes referred to as Old Jury – was the area populated by Jews in medieval London. Post-Fire, the parish was combined with the neighbouring St Martin Pomeroy and the new St Olave incorporated much of the walls and foundations of the earlier church buildings. The body of the church was rectangular, with shoulders on the western side narrowing to meet the tower, which was built separately and completed in 1679. The design of this 88-foot-tall tower is unusual for Wren in that it is the only one that narrows towards the top, a feature known architecturally as 'battered'. It is in three stages with a parapet and corner obelisks at the top, plus a sailing ship vane taken from St Mildred, Poultry. At its base there is the grand doorway flanked by Doric columns beneath a segmental pediment. Although dated 1824, the clock is a modern replacement for the original, which was sold with the church furnishings when St Olave was demolished in 1892 under the Union of Benefices Act. Only the tower, overlooking a small railed garden, and west wall survive and these have been incorporated within new buildings. The present offices were built in the 1980s and are occupied by a legal firm.

St Peters in Cornhil.

Unusually, the redbrick tower of St Peter upon Cornhill is finished with brick detailing on the surrounds and dressings. The main walls of the church are now stuccoed, creating an interesting contrast in building materials.

St Peter upon Cornhill

27 Survived. Location: Corner Cornhill and Gracechurch.

For St Peter upon Cornhill – one of the highest points within the city – Wren turned his well-tried formula of stone tower with brick body on its head, although strictly speaking the walls are stuccoed and not of stone. The dark brick on the tower is particularly distinctive in this instance as he utilised a lighter red brick instead of stone for window surrounds and dressings, and even for the upper stage. The leaded dome and the slender copper spire atop the tower are difficult to see from the churchyard garden on the south side – now a haven for displaced office smokers – and it can only be seen where it peeps up over the surrounding buildings. Wren Jnr described it as a 'plain solid church, from whence all ornament seems to have been purposefully banished', and while it may lack the usual excesses of English Baroque it is, nonetheless, a very pleasing building. 'Too much simplicity is a better fault than foolish ornament.' The interior is rich with dark woodwork, divided into four bays and the nave barrel-vaulted. You enter under the organ gallery and the walls are panelled up to the bottom of the round-headed windows. There is a chancel screen, reputedly designed by Wren's daughter, and a pulpit with weighty tester or sounding board above. The pews have gone, alas.

Restored in the 1980s, St Stephen Walbrook represents a very modern interpretation of Wren's work. Original features such as the canopied pulpit have been joined by Henry Moore's polished stone altar.

St Stephen Walbrook

28 Survived. Location: Walbrook.

The surviving Wren City churches, twenty-three if you don't count the lone towers or ruins, come in a variety of forms. Some are active places of worship while others are used for different purposes, some interiors possess great historical integrity while others have been modified or adapted to suit changing times. At first sight St Stephen Walbrook might appear to be in the latter category. This drastic restoration, conceived by Lord Polumbo and carried out in the 1980s, saw the old pews swept away and the layout changed to focus on a massive polished stone altar by Henry Moore. In the evening the interior, cited as one of Wren's finest, is bathed in warm electric light. I can only marvel at the result. The 63-foot-high dome is based on Wren's original design for St Paul's and is centred above a square of twelve Corinthian columns, from which eight arches spring to its circular base. The dome has a central lantern which reveals a delicious disk of blue sky. The tower is in four stages, the lower two of ragstone and the upper one dressed in Portland stone, with a succession of decreasing stone lanterns forming the steeple, possibly Hawksmoor's. Sir John Vanbrugh is buried here, and the Samaritans organisation was founded in the vestries in 1953 – the original telephone is displayed in a corner.

Almost abandoned as a ruin after the war, the interior of St Vedast-alias-Foster has been remodelled in a college chapel style.

St Vedast-alias-Foster

29 Blitzed, rebuilt. Location: Foster Lane.

Just along from St Mary-le-Bow, St Vedast in Foster Lane is dedicated to a French saint. The old church was not completely obliterated in the 1666 conflagration, but it did require substantial reconstruction, which took place between 1670–73. Wren incorporated parts of the surviving fabric and the tower was added in 1697, the spire in 1703. The body of the church is an unremarkable rectangle in plan and was described in *Parentalia* as 'well enlightened, but the windows irregular and raised to such a height that the doorways are under them'. The distinctive tower and spire have received mixed reviews. Wren Jnr called the spire 'low and heavy' while Betjeman says it is 'Wren's subtlest steeple', designed to contrast and not compete with St Mary-le-Bow. The church was gutted once more during the Blitz and, despite suggestions that it should be left in a ruined state as a memorial, it was restored by Stephen Dykes Bower. He reorganised the interior in a college chapel style with inward facing wooden seating or stalls down each side, and a side chapel tucked behind the backs of the south stalls. Other churches donated many of the furnishings, such as the pulpit from All Hallows, Bread Street, and the altarpiece from St Christopher-le-Stocks. It is a very pleasant interior, but it is not Wren.

All Hallows, Lombard Street

30 Moved to Twickenham. Original location: Corner Lombard Street and Gracechurch Street.

We now come to the case of the two missing churches. Gone, but not completely. All Hallows was sometimes known as the 'hidden church' as it was hemmed in by other buildings on Lombard Street. Contemporary engravings show Wren's post-Fire replacement as a very simple design with a rectangular body, lit by four round-headed windows along the side wall, and a plain 85-foot square tower in three stages. 'In the church is only one pillar, which, as also the pilasters, are of the Tuscan Order,' observed Wren Jnr. 'Length is 84ft, breadth 52ft and height about 30ft.' With a falling population by the early twentieth century the church was finally demolished in 1937. In an extraordinary example of recycling, the stone tower, porch, bells and furnishings were taken to a new site on Chertsey Road, Twickenham, where the tower was re-erected between 1939 and 1940. The main part of the new All Hallows – they kept the name – was designed by Robert Atkinson and is brick-built in a modern style and joined to the old tower by a cloister. The tower houses a peel of ten bells which were originally hung at St Dionis Backchurch before they went to Lombard Street. The original site of All Hallows on the corner of Lombard and Gracechurch Street is now occupied by offices.

The Parish Church of Alhallows Lombard Street

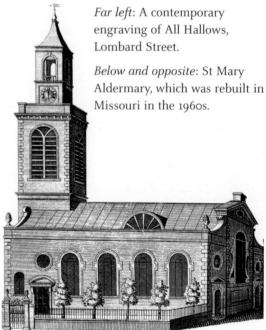

Far left: A contemporary engraving of All Hallows, Lombard Street.

Below and opposite: St Mary Aldermary, which was rebuilt in Missouri in the 1960s.

St Mary, Aldermanbury

③① Blitzed, remains of building moved to USA. Original location: Corner Aldermanbury and Love Lane.

For the other missing church, we have to travel much further afield than Twickenham. The original St Mary Aldermanbury dates back to the early twelfth century. Situated on the corner of Aldermanbury and Love Lane, it was rebuilt by Wren after the Great Fire, in 1677. We have Wren Jnr's description of a stone building with a 90-foot steeple, consisting of a tower and turret. The side walls featured four round-headed windows, a sturdy balustrade and an unusual semi-circular clerestory window into the roof space. The prominent east wall was typical Wren, with central pedimented gable and high, round-headed window flanked by smaller windows. Supported by twelve columns, the inside of the roof was adorned with arches of fretwork. The church was badly damaged by enemy action in 1940 and in 1966 the stones were taken to Fulton, Missouri, and the church rebuilt in the grounds of Westminster College as a memorial to Sir Winston Churchill. It was at Westminster College that Churchill made his famous 'Iron Curtain' speech in 1946. In London, the former site of the church has been planted to create the Aldermanbury Garden. It houses a large bust of William Shakespeare as a memorial to Henry Condell and John Hemmings, who lived in Aldermanbury and were instrumental in the production of the First Folio of his works.

Above: An observer scans the sky for enemy bombers in the early stages of the Second World War. (*NARA*)

Left: These markers on the wall of the Bank of England indicate old parish boundaries. Several of Wren's churches were demolished in the expansion of the Bank and the Royal Exchange.

The lost churches

In our heritage-conscious times it comes as a shock to discover that so many of Wren's City churches have been deliberately destroyed. Not just in the wanton destruction of the Blitz – the second Great Fire of London – but also through the actions of the Church itself. In the early part of the nineteenth century the population of the City had begun to decline and as the British Empire prospered, London became the conduit for its trade, creating increasing demand for commercial property and causing land prices to soar. In addition, the new railways were providing convenient transport to the outer reaches of London and thousands of tradesmen and craftsmen, who traditionally had worked above the premises, suddenly became commuters. The City's population of around 123,000 in the middle of the nineteenth century dwindled to only one-fifth that number by its end. This drift wasn't confined to the living, and in response to concerns about the health risk of burials in the City churchyards, many remains were re-interned in the new City of London Cemetery from 1856 onwards.

The Union of Benifices Act of 1860 enabled the Church authorities to dispose of the surplus churches, in theory using the money to build new ones elsewhere. The first to go was St Benet Gracechurch in 1868, followed by a succession of others: St Mildred, Poultry in 1872, St Antholin, Watling Street in 1874, St Michael Queenhithe in 1876, All Hallows, Bread Street and St Dionis, Backchurch in 1878, St Matthew, Friday Street in 1885, St Mary Magdalen, Old Fish Street in 1893 following a fire, All-Hallows-the-Great in 1894 and St Michael, Wood Street in 1897. Some were demolished for other reasons: St Christopher le Stocks in 1781 to provide space for the Bank of England, St Michael, Crooked Lane in 1831 to widen the approaches to London Bridge, St Bartholomew-by-the-Exchange in 1840 to widen Threadneedle Street, St Benet Fink in 1846 for the Royal Exchange, plus four declared as unsafe: St Michael Bassishaw in 1900, All Hallows, Lombard Street in 1937 (its tower rebuilt in Twickenham), and two with towers remaining, St Mary Somerset in 1871 and St Olave, Old Jewry in 1887.

During the Blitz just about every church suffered damage in some form or another and on one dreadful night in December 1940, eight Wren churches were burning. Many were rebuilt, but St Mildred Bread Street, St Stephen, Coleman and St Swithin, Cannon Street were not, while Christ Church Greyfriars, St Alban, Wood Street, St Augustine, Watling Street and St Dunstan-in-the-East were left as ruins or towers only. War-damaged St Mary, Aldermanbury, not demolished until 1966 was reconstructed at Fulton, Missouri, in the USA.

All Hallows, Bread Street

32 Demolished 1878. Location: Bread Street.

First mentioned in the thirteenth century, the pre-Fire 'Allhallows', Bread Street, is thought to have a Saxon foundation. In 1559 its steeple was brought down by lightning, killing a dog, and in 1608 John Milton was christened here. Post-Fire, it was rebuilt in 1684, although a new tower – by Hawksmoor – was only completed in 1698. The church had a plain body, slightly irregular in plan, with an annexe protruding to the south. The square tower was surmounted by a balustrade plus corner obelisks crowned with balls. After the Fire, the parish combined with St John the Evangelist, Friday Street, also destroyed but not rebuilt. Then in the late nineteenth century, it was joined with St Mary-le-Bow and the church was demolished in 1878.

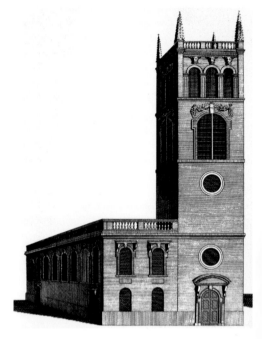

All-Hallows-the-Great

33 Demolished 1894. Location: Upper Thames Street.

All-Hallows, with the suffix 'Great' to distinguish it from nearby All-Hallows-the-Less, with which it combined after the Fire, was rebuilt between 1677 and 1684. The *Parentalia* describes the 87-foot-long church as being of 'considerable extent' and in very fine proportion. The exterior was quite plain, with round-headed windows. The tower, left standing after the Fire, had to be demolished and the molten bell metal was salvaged from the ruins to be recast into a new bell. The replacement tower was square with five stages and finished without spire or cupola. Together with the north aisle, it was demolished in 1876 to allow road widening. Another tower was constructed, on the south side, but the rest of the church was demolished in 1894. The tower survived until 1964.

St Antholin, Watling Street

34 Demolished 1874. Location: Watling Street.

Known variously as St Antony or St Antholin, Budge Row, after the original which stood on a street that no longer exists. A later church from the fifteenth century, described as 'expensively beautified' in 1616, was destroyed in the Fire and rebuilt 1678–1684. An engraving of the new church shows a square tower in two sections with a third octagonal top section and spire. Within the main body of the church, the roof space took the form of an elliptical cupola, illuminated via circular windows and supported on eight columns. St Antholin, Watling Street, was demolished in 1875 as a result of the Union of Benefices Act. A successor, St Antholin, Nunhead, was consecrated in 1878, destroyed in the Blitz and rebuilt in 2003 as St Anthony and St Silas.

Plaque on the wall of St Mary Aldermary.

St Bartholomew-by-the-Exchange

The Parish Church of St Bartholomew behind y^e Royal Exchange.

35 Demolished 1840. Location: Bartholomew Lane.

Formerly located on the east side of Bartholomew Lane, just off Threadneedle Street near the Royal Exchange, the old St Bartholomew was severely damaged in the Great Fire. The steeple was torn down in 1674 and rebuilding completed by 1683. The new church was described as 'a strong building, the roof flat, adorned with fretwork and supported with columns of the Tuscan Order and large arches', and it featured a 90-foot-tall square brick-built tower. However, this was an unlucky church and after the Royal Exchange burnt down in 1838, the Corporation of London obtained permission from Parliament to demolish it in order to widen Threadneedle Street. This was carried out in 1840 and the parish was combined with that of St Margaret Lothbury.

St Benet Fink

36 Demolished 1841–1846. Location: Threadneedle Street.

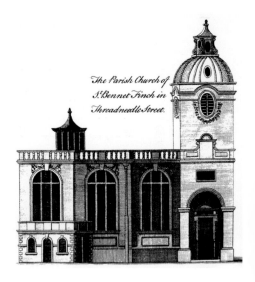

The Parish Church of S.'Bennet Finch in Threadneedle Street.

St Benedict, to be correct, was located on what is now Threadneedle Street. The Fink part of the name was derived from Robert Fink, a thirteenth-century benefactor. Following the Great Fire it was rebuilt in 1670, although some of the land had been appropriated by the City to widen Threadneedle Street. This left an irregular site which Wren filled with a decagonal layout for the main body of the church with six tall, curve-headed windows and capped with an oval dome or cupola. The 110-foot tower, on the west side, featured a square dome and bell cage. St Benet Fink was knocked down in stages as part of improvements made following a fire at the Royal Exchange, with full demolition taking place in 1846.

St Benet Gracechurch

37 Demolished 1868. Location: Junction Gracechurch and Fenchurch Street.

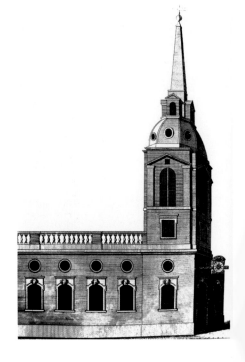

Another St Benet, this time with the suffix Gracechurch or 'Grass Church' after the nearby hay market. The post-Fire structure was relatively small, only 60 feet long in the main section, and was described as a well-proportioned and 'handsome' church. The rectangular body of the church was illuminated via two rows of windows, with arched oblongs on the lower level and a series of portholes above. A balustrade ran along either side of the roof. Above the square tower the steeple consisted of a lead-covered dome, again with portholes, topped by a slender obelisk spire. St Benet was demolished in 1868 to allow for the widening of Gracechurch Street. The furnishings were redistributed among other churches and the pulpit went to St Olave in Hart Street.

St Christopher le Stocks

38 Demolished 1782. Location: Threadneedle Street.

St Christopher was one of the City's oldest churches and may have dated from the thirteenth century. It was situated on the south side of Threadneedle Street and the suffix, le Stocks, might refer to the nearby city stocks. After the Fire Wren rebuilt the church in 1671, using much of the surviving material and incorporating parts of the walls not destroyed, which may be why it was one of the first to be completed. The contemporary engravings show a small-bodied building with a comparatively tall square tower of about 80 feet. The church was demolished in 1782 to provide space for the extension of the Bank of England, and a parish boundary mark can be seen on the front wall of the bank.

St Dionis, Backchurch

39 Demolished 1878. Location: Philpot Lane.

Not all of Wren's churches were regarded as great architecture. In 1858, the *Civil Engineers and Architects Journal* described St Dionis as 'one of the most commonplace and ugly of the many churches rebuilt after the Great Fire'. This observation might have been coloured by the rise of Victorian Gothic, but with some of the lesser churches it is clear that Wren's office hadn't over-exerted their talents. St Dionis Backchurch, so named because it stood back behind the shops on Fenchurch Street, was rebuilt in 1674 with a short steeple or turret, which raised the height to 90 feet, added ten years later. Unloved and unappreciated, it was one of the first churches to join with another parish under the Union of Benefices Act 1860.

St George, Botolph Lane

40 Demolished 1904. Location: Botolph Lane.

St George was on the west side of Botolph
Lane, backing on to Pudding Lane at the seat
of the Great Fire. In the aftermath the parish
was combined with St Botolph Billingsgate,
also destroyed in the blaze, and rebuilding
commenced in 1671 using rubble from the
old St Paul's and stone for the walls recovered
from St Botolph. Completed in 1676, the Wren
church was roughly square with the interior
divided into nave and aisles by four columns.
The tower, incorporated within the north-west
corner of the building, was topped with a
parapet of flaming urns. By the late nineteenth
century the church had fallen into decay and
was condemned as structurally unsafe. It closed
in 1901 and was taken down three years later.

St Mary Magdalen, Old Fish Street

41 Demolished 1893. Location: Old Fish Street.

Roughly rectangular, this was a small but well
proportioned church. It had round-headed
windows, four on the south front and three
on the east. These were so high up that the
entrance was situated beneath them. Its walls
were surmounted by a modest balustrade, and
the tower capped by an unusual octagonal
pyramid of stone steps on which sat a lantern
and short steeple. Rather than a weathervane
there was a finial in the form of an urn,
alluding to Mary Magdalen's pot of balm.
In 1886, a fire in a neighbouring warehouse
damaged the roof and as several city churches
were being pulled down at the time, under the
Union of Benefices Act 1860, the church was
demolished and the parish combined with
St Martin Ludgate.

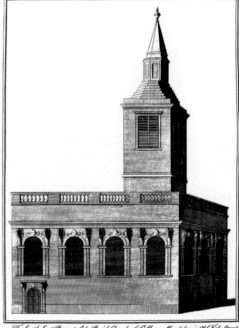

The South East Prospect of the Parish Church of St Mary Magdalen in Old Fish Street.

St Matthew, Friday Street

42 Demolished 1885. Location: Friday Street, off Cheapside.

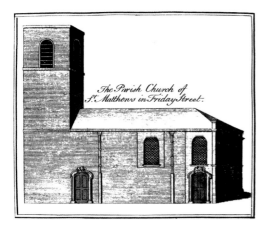

Appropriately enough for a church dedicated to the patron saint of accountants, this was the plainest of Wren's designs and the cheapest. Completed in 1685, it was based on an irregular rectangle with walls of rubble and only the visible east wall, onto Friday Street, faced with stone. Unadorned at street level, it had a row of five round headed windows. The tower was equally plain as it was not visible from the street and housed a solitary bell. Redundant by the late nineteenth century, it was demolished in 1885 and the parish joined to St Vedast-alias-Foster. During the Blitz, Friday Street itself was destroyed and the site was built over in the 1950s, and in this perpetually changing city it is being redeveloped once again.

St Michael Bassishaw

43 Demolished 1900. Location: Basinghall Street.

'Bassishaw' is a combination of a prominent local family name, 'Basing', and 'haw', meaning yard. A church dedicated to the Archangel Michael had stood here since the twelfth century. Reconstruction after the Fire started in 1675. The octagonal steeple, surmounted by a lantern, is probably the work of Robert Hooke. The church was poorly built, with insufficient foundations, and 'made up of several sorts of materials and plastered over'. By 1693 the parish was lobbying Wren's office to make repairs. This was done in 1713 when parts of the upper walls were rebuilt, the slate roof replaced with lead and a tower added. The latter was topped by a short spire terminating with a ball. Demolished in 1900, the site is now underneath the Barbican.

St Michael, Crooked Lane

44 Demolished 1831. Location: Miles' Lane.

Another very old church, St Michael was located on the east side of Miles Lane, Great Eastcheap, in Candlewick Ward. It was here that the first cases of plague occurred in 1665, the year before the Great Fire destroyed it. According to Christopher Wren Jnr, it was rebuilt in 1688 in stone. However, in 1831 this ill-fated church was demolished to make way in order to widen the approaches to the rebuilt London Bridge. It was united with St Magnus the Martyr, which itself was altered because of the bridge, and it is at St Magnus that a representation of St Michael Crooked Lane can be found in a commemorative stained glass window. This shows an elegant stone tower around 100 feet high and topped with pinnacles.

St Michael, Crooked Lane, commemorated in a stained glass window at St Magnus the Martyr.

St Michael, Queenhithe

45 Demolished 1876. Location: Upper Thames Street.

First recorded in the twelfth century, the church was named after St Michael the Arch Angel and located in the ward of Queenhithe, on what is now Upper Thames Street, roughly where the footbridge crosses near St James Galickhythe. Post-Fire, it was rebuilt between 1676 and 1686 with stone walls, flattish roof and a slender tower with stone steps capped by a tall spire. Its main front, on the south and east facing the Queenhithe docks, featured familiar Wren motifs with five round-topped windows and portholes above separated by decorative swags. The weathervane, in the form of a three-masted barque, is now on St Nicholas Cole Abbey. Another victim of the population drift away from central London, St Michael Queenhithe was demolished in 1875.

The Parish Church of St. Michael's Queenhythe

St Michael, Wood Street

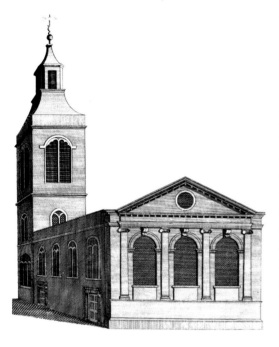

46 Demolished 1897. Location: Wood Street.

Another church dedicated to the Arch Angel Michael. Situated on the west side of Wood Street, Wren Jnr described it as plain 'but with a great deal of symmetry'. The east end had three large, round-topped windows separated by a series of Ionic pillars crowned with a triangular pediment, giving it the flavour of a Greek temple. The sides featured high windows with the doors under them, and at the western end a square tower in three stages beneath a concave curved roof supporting a short turret. It was demolished in 1897 under the Union of Benefices Act and the parish united with St Alban Wood Street. In turn, when that church was destroyed in the Blitz, the parish was joined with St Vedast Foster Lane.

St Mildred Bread Street

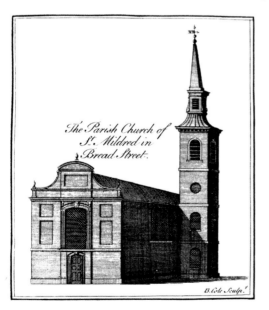

The Parish Church of S.ᵗ Mildred in Bread Street.

B. Cole Sculp.ᵗ

47 Blitzed 1940–41. Location: Bread Street.

Dating back to the thirteenth century, the church burnt down in 1666, was rebuilt by Wren and then destroyed in the 1940–41 Blitz. Engravings show an elegant structure, the front on to Bread Street built in stone and the remainder, including the tower, in brick. Unusually, each side of the main body of the church had a large single window. The tower on the south-east corner was in four stages, very slender overall and had a sleek spire pointing 140 feet into the London sky. The poet Percy Bsyche Shelley married his second wife, Mary Godwin, at St Mildred's in 1816. As Mary Shelley, she is best known for her Gothic novel *Frankenstein or The Modern Prometheus*, which was published two years later.

St Mildred, Poultry

48 Demolished 1872. Location: Poultry.

Although a small church, only 56 feet long and 42 feet wide, Wren's design for St Mildred Poultry was very distinctive, with strong cornice and pediment detailing offset by delicate 'enrichments and foliage' cut in stone. The roof was flat, the squat tower unembellished by the usual spire or dome. Sadly, nothing remains; the church which was rebuilt after the Great Fire between 1670–1676 was sold off in 1871. It was demolished the following year and the land redeveloped. A plaque on the corner of Poultry and Mansion House Street in Cheap commemorates the site. The sixteenth-century poet Thomas Tusser was buried at the old church in 1580. His writings are the source of the proverb, ' A fool and his money are soon parted.'

South View of St Mildred's Church in the Poultry.

St Stephen, Coleman

49 Blitzed 1940. Location: Corner Coleman Street and Gresham Street.

Another of Wren's churches lost in the Blitz – it had been previously damaged by bombings in 1917 – St Stephen was located at the corner of what is now Gresham Street, with the main façade on Coleman Street. This was faced in Portland stone and embellished by a semi-circular pediment between two pineapples. Wren Jnr described the body of the church as 'plain and solid', strengthened with rusticated corners. 'The windows are large, and one series of them very well enlightens it. In the east end they are larger than the rest, but of the same form.' The 85-foot tower, on the north-west, was almost hidden from the street with just the bell lantern and gilded vane visible above the flat roof.

The South East Prospect of the Parish Church of St Stephen Coleman Street

100   200   300   400   500

B. Cole sculp.

St Swithin, Cannon Street

The Parish Church of St. Swithin, in Cannon Street.

50 Blitz damaged, demolished 1962. Location: Cannon Street.

Sometimes known as St Swithin London Stone, the church was founded in the thirteenth century, rebuilt in 1405, and lost in the Great Fire of 1666. Situated on the north side of Cannon Street, it was rebuilt by Wren in 1679 in stone and had a plain tower capped by a balustrade enclosing the base of a tall spire, giving an overall height of 150 feet. Inside, the church featured three aisles, with the roof supported by demi-columns. Despite being quite small, it was described as an 'elegant and commodious building'. Unfortunately, it was badly damaged in an air raid in 1940 and finally demolished in 1962. Today, only a small garden of remembrance marks the site, and this is now known as Walbrook Gardens.

The view across the Thames, *c.* 1900, with The Monument and the tower of St Magnus the Martyr on the far side of London Bridge. (*LoC*)

One of the best views of St Paul's Cathedral
is from the London Millennium Bridge.

St Paul's Cathedral

For 300 years Christopher Wren's great cathedral has dominated the skyline of London. It is his masterpiece and his monument. The present St Paul's is the fifth to stand on Ludgate Hill, the highest point in the capital. The original church was founded in 604 and the next two successors burnt down, in 962 and in 1087. It was the fourth incarnation, the medieval cathedral started by the Normans and consecrated in 1300, that Wren would have first encountered. Old St Paul's, as it has become known, was the third longest church in Europe and its central spire of 489 feet was one of the tallest. However, in 1561 the mighty spire was destroyed by a lightning strike and by the mid-sixteenth century St Paul's had fallen into disrepair. As early as 1661 Wren had been advising on the repairs and, shortly before the Great Fire of 1666, he had even produced drawings for a dome to replace the missing spire. Although Old St Paul's was gutted in the terrible conflagration, initially it was thought that the ruins might be workable, but by the early 1670s the decision had been taken to demolish the entire structure and build anew.

Wren's designs for St Paul's went through five general stages or schemes. The first, produced in 1669, was known as the First Model – after the practice of presenting designs in the form of wooden scale models – and had a round domed entrance vestibule leading into a rectangular basilica. This was rejected as being too modest and not 'stately enough', which probably meant it had too much of a Roman flavour at a time when the nation was still suffering a religious identity crisis. His next design was based on a Greek cross – one where the four branches are of equal length – the main interior centralised beneath a dome and subsidiary spaces arranged around the sides. This was far too radical for the clergy. On the third design, the Great Model, unveiled in 1673, Wren extended the nave as a concession towards the preferred Latin cross floor-plan, still with a dome. This was Wren's personal favourite and despite the critics, who bemoaned the fact that it looked too different from existing English churches, he resolved not to make any more models or to expose his drawings to 'incompetent judges'. Accordingly, he fell back on the old designers' trick of presenting the client with one design while intending to produce another. In the 'Warrant' design, his fourth, he appears to have deliberately over-egged the brief by producing a long nave, flanked by lower aisles, with a pagoda-like half dome half spire that evoked the great churches of medieval England.

The Warrant design was approved by Charles II and work commenced in the summer of 1675. But Wren had his own agenda and he persuaded the king to allow him 'some variations, rather ornamental, than essential, as from time to time he should see proper'. Like a magician, he would sometimes screen the workings from public gaze and the building that eventually emerged differed radically from the Warrant design, not least with the return of the high dome from the Great Model. Structurally challenging, the dome is a clever piece of architectural sleight-of-hand with triple domes, one inside the other like a Russian doll. At its core is a steep parabolic cone of brick which provides the structural support for the heavy stone spire at the top. This is hidden from view externally by an outer cone or shell supported on a timber frame, and on the inside by the lower painted dome. When you stand in the nave looking up there is a circular opening at the crown which reveals what appears to be a cylindrical space, but this is actually the underside of the brick dome painted with architectural detail in false perspective. The inner dome is adorned with eight monochrome

Looking up into the interior of the great dome of St Paul's Cathedral. This is actually the underside of three domes sitting one inside the other. (*Johnny Greig*)

paintings by Sir James Thornhill depicting the life of St Paul. There are two galleries; the Golden Gallery is at the top of the brick cone, 280 feet above ground level, and below the base of the cone, a mere 99 feet and 259 steps from ground level, there is the famous Whispering Gallery, noted for the acoustic effect which enables a listener with an ear to the wall to hear a whisper from the far side.

The dome is restrained around its base by a wrought iron chain to prevent spread and cracking, and there are further chains at intervals in the brick cone. The walls of the cathedral are particularly thick, eliminating the external buttresses of the Warrant design, and the upper parts of the cathedral are reinforced with flying buttresses, which were added at a relatively late stage, for extra strength. These are concealed behind a screen wall to maintain the building's classical lines.

The cathedral is 574 feet long including the portico of the Great West Door, the nave is 121 feet wide and, including the transepts, the overall

Left: West front of St Paul's Cathedral. One tower houses the bells and the other a clock. (*LoC*)
Above: Statue of Queen Anne in front of the west front. (*Man vyi*)

width is 246 feet. The west front consists of the two-storey colonnaded portico beneath a triangular pediment. Two imposing towers rise to either side, the southern one with a clock and the north one containing thirteen bells, including the massive St Paul bell, which at 16.5 tons is the largest in the UK. For the main body Wren created a two-storey façade with rows of windows and/or niches, although by the latter part of the build his grip on the project was slipping and an unnecessary balustrade was added along the parapet of the nave.

St Paul's Cathedral came into use in December 1697, and was officially completed in 1710 when, at the age of seventy-six, Sir Christopher Wren watched his son fix the last stone in place on the lantern at the top of the great dome. In medieval times a cathedral was the work of generations, spanning hundreds of years, but Wren's great masterpiece was completed in under forty years. Even so, by the time of Wren's death his style of architecture was already out of favour. He died on 25 February 1723 at the age of ninety, and his remains were placed in the crypt of his beloved cathedral. Beneath the dome a stone plaque bears an inscription penned by his son. Translated from the Latin it reads:

Here in its foundations lies the architect of this church and city, Christopher Wren, who lived beyond ninety years, not for his own profit but for the public good. Reader, if you seek his monument – look around you.

When London faced its darkest hours during the Blitz, Wren's cathedral came to symbolise the nation's faith in its own survival. It was struck by enemy bombs on several occasions and on the night of 29 December, there was a vicious rain of incendiaries that set half of London alight. Churchill sent word that the cathedral should be saved at all costs. At around nine o'clock in the evening it was hit by a fire-bomb which burnt through the lead roof and wooden timbers and then dislodged to fall on the nave below where, thankfully, it could be dealt with. The poignant photograph of the dome of St Paul's Cathedral shrouded in billowing smoke has become one of the defining images of the twentieth century.

Opposite: As London burned during the air raids of December 1940, St Paul's Cathedral shone through the clouds of billowing smoke as a symbol of hope in the dark days of the Second World War. (*NARA*)

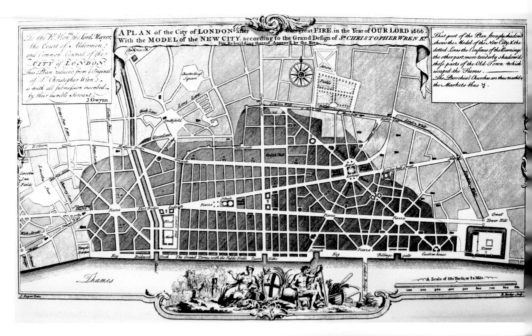

A PLAN of the City of LONDON after the great FIRE in the Year of OUR LORD 1666. With the MODEL of the NEW CITY, according to the Grand Design of Sᵗ CHRISTOPHER WREN Kᵗ. For Rebuilding thereof. Approved by the King.

Above: Wren's plans for a reborn London.

Below: The Monument to the Great Fire (Cornell University), and shown right, its spiral staircase.

Bottom right: St James's Church.

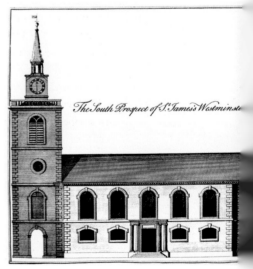

The South Prospect of Sᵗ James's Westminster

Wren's Other London

In the aftermath of the Great Fire, Wren saw an opportunity for the City to be completely rebuilt, starting from scratch to a far more organised plan. He envisioned a grand piazza west of the River Fleet and to the east a new St Paul's at the meeting point of two broad avenues. The muddle of the old streets and alleyways would be swept away to be replaced by an ordered grid arrangement with wide streets running north–south and roughly east to west. Wren was not alone in his vision for a reborn city and, encouraged by the king, several equally grand schemes were submitted by John Evelyn, Robert Hooke, Valentine Knight and Richard Newcourt. None came to fruition as the whole business of establishing who owned each individual plot of land and negotiating compensation, not to mention the practicalities of rebuilding an entire city, was far too complicated and expensive. In the actual rebuilding, some streets were widened to improve fire safety and hygiene, and the new buildings were of brick and stone rather than wood. However, with the exception of King Street and Queen Street, the thoroughfares still largely follow the old medieval plan to this day, and the public buildings, including the cathedral, churches and so on, were rebuilt on their previous sites.

The Monument

One new structure to rise out of the ashes was a permanent memorial to the Great Fire. The Monument, designed by Christopher Wren and Robert Hooke, takes the form of a fluted Doric column 202 feet high – a figure chosen as it marks the distance to the spot in Pudding Lane where the fire started. Constructed between 1671 and 1677 of Portland stone, it is the tallest free-standing column in the world, and capped by a gilded urn of fire, it once towered over this part of London before the epidemic of modern office buildings began to crowd in. The best thing about The Monument is that it is hollow and a narrow cantilevered staircase of 311 steps leads visitors to a viewing platform near the top. Wren and Hooke also utilised this vertical shaft as a scientific instrument, both as a zenith telescope – a fixed one looking straight up – and for use in gravity and pendulum experiments with an underground laboratory beneath the base of the stairs and a hinged lid on the top of the urn. Furthermore, the steps, at six-inch intervals, could be used for observations of variations in barometric pressure. The Monument cost a little over £13,450 to construct, and more recently it has undergone a major £4.5 million restoration. The views are breathtaking, and so is the climb.

Not affected by the Great Fire, St Clement Danes on Fleet Street was rebuilt by Wren between 1680 and 1682.

Other London churches

In addition to those within the old City walls, Wren designed a number of other churches in London. Located on The Strand, St Clement Danes is known as one of the two 'island churches' – the other being St Mary-le-Strand – named because the road passes on either side. A church has stood here for over a thousand years, going back to the Danes in the ninth century, and was rebuilt by William the Conqueror and again in medieval times. By the late seventeenth century, St Clement Danes was in a terrible state and Wren was tasked with rebuilding it between 1680 and 1682, with the 115-foot tower added in 1720 by James Gibbs. During the Blitz in 1941 it was hit by fire bombs and totally gutted, and following an appeal by the Royal Air Force, it was restored by 1958 and subsequently became the Central Church of the RAF. Statues of the RAF's wartime leaders Hugh Dowding and, more controversially, Arthur 'Bomber' Harris, stand in the church grounds to mark this association. There are further RAF-related memorials inside the church itself. St Clement Danes is said to be the church featured in the children's rhyme, 'Oranges and lemons say the bells of St Clements', although St Clement Eastcheap is also a contender for this honour.

Further west there are two more Wren-connected churches – St James's Church, Piccadilly and St Anne's Church, Soho – both of which were built as new churches. Commissioned in 1672 and constructed at roughly the same time as the City churches, St James's is a typical Wren design, in the

Left: Interior of The Temple Church, which was modified by Wren.

Right: Temple Bar, the former gateway into the City and now re-sited as an entrance into Paternoster Square.

vein of St Andrew-by-the-Wardrobe or St Andrew, Holborn, with walls of dark red brick and Portand stone dressings. The body of this large parish church is rectangular with two rows of round-headed windows along the sides and, inside, galleries on three sides supported on Corinthian pillars, plus a fine barrel-vaulted ceiling above the naive. It is said to accommodate up to 2,000 people, causing Wren to comment, 'I can hardly think to make a single room so spacious, as to hold 2,000 persons, and all to hear the service, and both to hear distinctly and see the preacher.' The square tower in three stages is capped by a lead sheathed lantern and spire. Grinling Gibbons carved the fine marble font and wooden reredos. The church was gutted in the Blitz but has since been restored.

St Anne's Church, Soho, is on a similar layout. However, the original tower had to be demolished in 1800 because it had become unstable and a new one was completed in 1803. Another victim of the Blitz, the church was not fully restored until the early 1990s.

Temple Church and Temple Bar

Wren also had a hand in the refurbishment or 'reordering' of The Temple Church, which is famed for its circular nave – modelled on the Holy Sepulchre in Jerusalem and known as 'the round' – and an appearance in Dan Brown's *The Da Vinci Code*. Situated on the far west side of the City and hidden among the alleyways between Fleet Street and the Thames,

Above: Wren reorientated Kensington Palace with a new entrance and façade.
Below: Typical Wren detailing on the Royal Apartments at Hampton Court. (*Man vyi*)

The Temple Church narrowly escaped the flames of 1666. However, it was extensively modified by Wren, who added an altar-screen and organ, both of which were destroyed by fire during the Blitz.

Temple Church and the immediate area takes its name from Temple Bar, the boundary where the westernmost extent of the City meets Westminster, and Fleet Street becomes The Strand. Historically this was more than just a symbolic boundary, as it denoted the extent of the City of London Corporation's powers. When it was decided to replace the medieval wooden archway after the Great Fire, King Charles II commissioned Wren to design a new arch of Portland stone. Constructed between 1669 and 1672, it consisted of a wide central arch, with smaller ones for pedestrians on either side, beneath a decorative pediment with niches occupied by statues of Queen Anne of Denmark and James I on the eastern face, and looking outwards on the other side were Charles I and Charles II. Wren's arch stood at Temple Bar for 200 years until pressure to widen the road saw its removal to a country estate in Hertfordshire. It returned to London in 2004 and, thoroughly spruced up, it now serves an entranceway into the redeveloped Paternoster Square, on the north side of St Paul's.

Royal Hospital Chelsea

As Surveyor of the Kings Works from 1669 to 1718, Wren designed a number of secular buildings. The first large scale commission came in 1681, when King Charles II issued a Royal Warrant authorising the building of the Royal Hospital Chelsea on a site overlooking the Thames. This was to be a home for old or injured soldiers and Wren's design featured a pair of four-storey quadrangles on either side of a central court – Figure Court – opening to the south, and all in perfect symmetry. The grand colonnaded portico reaches up to the level of the rooftop and rising above it is one of Wren's signature octagonal cupolas and lanterns. The Chelsea Pensioners are accommodated in the Long Wards in 'berths' which have the look and feel of well-appointed cupboards. Originally Wren had allowed just 6 feet square for each individual berth, but in the 1950s they were enlarged to the present 9 feet square and a current refurbishment programme will greatly improve upon this. The chapel is contained within the central joining section and in the half dome and apse it features a spectacular painting of the Resurrection by Sebastiano Ricci.

Greenwich Observatory and Royal Hospital

Commissioned by King Charles II in 1675, the Royal Observatory at Greenwich was the first purpose-built scientific research facility in

Above: The Greenwich Observatory, which was built on foundations of the old castle.

Main picture: One of the great towers on the Royal Hospital for Seamen. Wren's grand symmetrical design at Greenwich repeats many of the architectural elements to be found on St Paul's Cathedral. (*CMc*

the country. Wren had an intense interest in all branches of science, including optics and astronomy, and he designed the observatory, probably with the assistance of Robert Hooke. It was built at the top of the hill on the foundations of a tower which had been part of the old Greenwich Castle. As a result, it was aligned thirteen degrees away from true north, much to the annoyance of the Astronomer Royal, John Flamsteed.

Also in Greenwich, in 1694 the Royal Hospital for Seamen was founded as a residential home for injured sailors on the instructions of Queen Mary II. Originally the plan was to modify a wing of Greenwich Palace to accommodate the hospital, but when the Queen discovered that this might obstruct her riverside views, it was decided that a new building was required and the old dilapidated palace was demolished in 1694. Two years later, Wren was appointed as Surveyor of Greenwich Naval Hospital and, assisted by Nicholas Hawksmoor, he drew up plans for a split layout consisting of four blocks of buildings arranged around quadrants and bisected north–south. Wren and Hawksmoor gave their services free, and after Wren's death in 1723, Sir John Vanburgh completed the hospital complex to Wren's original designs. Knowing that he would not live to see the completion of the building, Wren cannily insisted on laying the foundations first to prevent others from changing his layout. It was not finished completely until 1752. Greenwich Hospital closed in 1869 and between 1873 and 1998 it was occupied by the Admiralty as the Royal Naval College. Today, it is part of the Maritime Greenwich World Heritage Site – awarded by UNESCO in 1997 – which includes the National Maritime Museum in the former 1807 school building, plus the Queen's House and Royal Observatory.

Morden College

Continuing on the theme of almshouses, Morden College in Kidbrooke Gardens, Greenwich, was founded by the philanthropist Sir John Morden for 'decayed Turkey Merchants' – presumably the merchants were decayed, and not the turkeys. Built between 1695 and 1702, Wren's design is a low, wide structure in red brick with stone dressings, laid out to form a quadrangle within. It is another fine example of his love of formal symmetry and the grand entrance is reminiscent of his other works. An imposing oak doorway sits beneath a curved pediment on Doric columns to either side. Looking like a mantelpiece clock, the central bay extends forwards slightly and is capped by a wide triangular pediment with a double niche for the statues of Sir John and Lady Morden (later additions), the whole capped by an elegant clock tower. The building still serves as almshouses.

The Royal Palaces

Wren naturally had responsibility for work on the Royal palaces. When William and Mary wanted to move from the notoriously damp Westminster Palace to a new home in Kensingston – a grand house formerly known as Nottingham House – they called in their man to make a number of improvements. Most notably, Wren added pavilions or blocks to the four corners, each one with three storeys and attics above, and he re-orientated the building by creating a new entrance and service courtyard, the Great Court, on the western side. The Royal Court took up residence in 1689 and further alterations followed.

The king also wanted Wren to rebuild Hampton Court Palace, the original intention being to demolish the Tudor palace a section at a time and to build anew from scratch. In the event, money was not available for a wholesale 'Wrenovation' and he was restricted instead to rebuilding the Royal Apartments on the south and east side with Versailles-inspired façades, consisting of row upon row of sash windows against redbrick, that dominate the formal gardens. Work at Hampton Court Palace commenced in 1689, with Wren being assisted by William Talman as

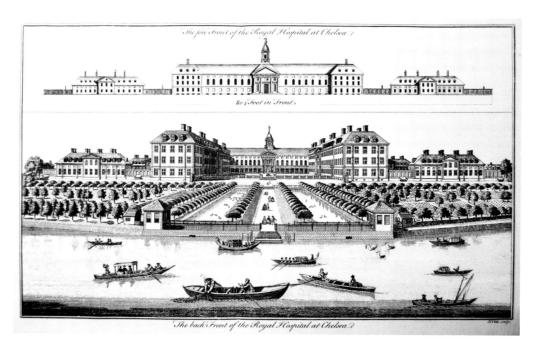

The fore Front of the Royal Hospital at Chelsea

80 Foot in Front

The back Front of the Royal Hospital at Chelsea

Master of Works. Following Queen Mary's early death from smallpox in 1694 at the age of thirty-two, King William lost interest in the work at Hampton Court. Ironically, it was here in 1702 that the king fell from his horse and he was taken to Kensington, where he died shortly afterwards.

Other works

Both Wrens, father and son, worked on Marlborough House, which was built for Sarah Churchill, Duchess of Marlborough, and completed in 1711. Situated in Pall Mall, to the east of St James's Palace, this is a fairly plain building of red brick with characteristic stone quoins. The original had only two storeys, topped by a balustrade with corner urns. Between 1861 and 1863 Sir James Pennethorne made a number of alterations for the Prince of Wales, who lived there until he became King Edward VII, and these included two additional attic storeys.

Wren has also been credited with several other London buildings, including the Trinity Hospital almshouses in Mile End Road, founded 1695, and the rebuilding of the Drury Lane Theatre in 1674. But just as with the City churches, the extent of his involvement is hotly contested among some experts, although in the case of Trinity Hospital it does have a lot in common with his other buildings.

Opposite: Marlborough House in Pall Mall, built for Sarah Churchill, Duchess of Marlborough. (*C Mallwitz*). *Above*: The Royal Hospital at Chelsea was Wren's first large scale commission from the king.

Further reading

Building St Paul's, by James W. P. Campbell, Thames & Hudson, 2008.
City Churches of Sir Christopher Wren, by Paul Jeffery, Hambledon Continuum, 2007.
City of London Churches, by John Betjeman, Pitkin Publishing, 2009.
London: The City Churches, by Simon Bradley and Nikolaus Pevsner, Yale University Press, 2002.
Parentalia – Memoirs of the Family of the Wrens, by Christopher Wren (his son), London 1750, facsimile printed by the Cregg Press in 1965.
Wren, by Margaret Whinney, Thames & Hudson, 1985.

Acknowledgements

I would like to thank Campbell McCutcheon (CMcC), of Amberley Publishing, for commissioning this book and for supplying several pictures from his extensive collection of old postcards. For additional images I am grateful to the US Library of Congress (LoC) and US National Archives (NARA), Gren, Yulia Belousova/Dreamstime, John Armagh, Dragos Daniel Iliescu/Dreamstime, Johnny Greig, Man Vyi, C. Mallwitz, Tony Hisgett and Cornell University Library. Unless otherwise credited, all new photography is by the author (JC). I must also thank my wife Ute for proof reading and patience.